Nothing Louche

Tina C
&
Michael W. Thomas

Nothing Louche or Bohemian

First published in 2025 by Black Pear Press
Copyright © Tina Cole & Michael W. Thomas 2025
All rights reserved.

No part of this publication may be reproduced, copied, stored in a retrieval system, or transmitted in any form or by any means without prior permission in writing from the copyright holder. Nor may it be otherwise circulated in any form or binding or cover other than the one in which it is published and without conditions including this condition being imposed on subsequent purchasers.

All the characters in this publication, other than those clearly in the public domain, are fictitious and any resemblance to real persons, living or dead, is purely coincidental.

ISBN 978-1-916910-27-0

Design and Layout: Black Pear Press

Black Pear Press

Dedication

To those people and places that, for good or ill, have haunted our rear-view mirror.

Introduction

It's been said that, when you remember something, you're not actually recalling it afresh. Instead, you're remembering the last time you remembered it. On this reckoning, memories are like copies from a printer whose ink is giving out. Whether or not the theory is true, the people, scenes and episodes in this collection are remarkably tenacious. In one form or another, they have travelled along with Tina and me through more years than…well, hot dinners come to mind. And writing about them, we felt they were as sharp as the day they happened to us. Here are keepsakes stowed any old how in a box. Here are wise words imparted to one impressionable mind, while another such mind confects fantasies from an overheard phone call. Here are the coping-tiles of an estate crescent, then the bend of an almost country road bracketed off from sub-suburbia. Here are the seemingly endless depths of the local Baths. Most of all, here are the people who have insisted on sharing all our years with us. Reading this collection, you may have the sense of faces, times and emotions rearing up at you as in 3-D. This is certainly how Tina and I felt, which is why we sought to shuffle, pair and order them—not in a deadeningly formal way, but with some sense of themes…as you might place stamps, fairly tidily, in an album. Stamp albums…the Stanley Gibbons Catalogue comes to mind. He's not here, but Knight's Castile Soap is, with Brooke Bond Orange Label Tea and Pepsodent…just three of the clamorous runes on our back pages.

Tina Cole and Michael W. Thomas (January 2025)

Contents

Introduction	i
Contents	ii
Open the Box	1
Dad in a Morning—December 1962	3
Sunday Morning	5
These I have Loved	6
Pit Fodder	7
Ivyhouse Junction	8
Many Mansions	9
Intoxication	11
Earless	12
Heirloom	14
Unmapped	15
Baggeridge Wood	16
Cats Fed	17
Dog Collar	19
Jacqueline Burnett	20
Sally Riordan	21
Mrs MacIntyre	22
Piano Teacher	23
Diana Ingall	24
What Granny Hayden had to Say	26
Somersault	27
All the Light	29
Swimming Lesson Coseley Baths 1961	31
The Art of Knitting	32
Local Vagrant Dudley 1960's	33
Pity Phones	34
Canal Bridge 236—Betsy's Tale	35
Wyndham the Fuse: it Sure is	36
Authors	38
Acknowledgements	40
Reviews	41

Open the Box

This is for you, you said and gave me a box
weighty as lead, steel-banded with no key
at least none I could find, perhaps it was lost
in time inside some great chest. I sensed
only its heft, something locked and kept for years.
You said, *here are the lessons I learned by heart.*

(Certainly, I needed to better know your heart).
I have gathered them together in this box,
shifting moods, quickening fears hidden for years.
In that moment I was glad there wasn't a key
no need to gloss the mad daily stand, the sense
of win, lose, no Pandora release of loss.

The box found a high shelf. I tried not to lose
myself in regret, just kept contorting my heart
until I found some understanding, a sense
of grace and pleasure in the world. I too boxed
it up, work another day was always the key.
Mind the gaps. Mind the cracks. Wait out the years,

(who knows what for?) Don't let's review them year
by year, the sometimes shards of brilliance, jewels lost
then found. Small splinters of certitude, old keys
in Gold Flake tins, thank God the chambers of the heart
continued banging that necessary boom box
beat. Yet still too often, *I'm not so sure,* my senses

said. Oh, let's just stand side by side in sensible
shoes, my hand, your hand, all those complicated years
stuffed in a Tesco bag, step over empty boxes
littering the market square, rotting fruits, profits lost.
It's not rocket science, the butcher has hearts
and chicken wings. The hardware shops have keys.

Permit yourself anger, permit me mine, no key
or lock is necessary. Common sense
should prevail. Nothing needs to fail, not faith nor heart,
even see-saws level after many rusting years.
It's extraordinary that nothing is lost
perhaps balance is what we should lock in a box?

At last, perhaps we get it, the key to contented years,
in a sense we knew all along, but somehow we lost
the bigger picture of the heart and ended up with trinkets in a box.

Dad in a Morning—December 1962

Wyndham Thomas, John Thompson (Boiler Makers) Ltd,
Ettingshall Road, Wolverhampton, 1957-1973

And so he shoulders open
the door of his Thames van,
ready, even on Christmas Eve,
to head for the factory
whose overhead piazzas
and valleys of wire
need his sparky magic
to keep all on the pulse.

Only now, years later, do I wonder
how he kept his head distracted
as the dawn roads of Coseley
gave way to Bilston's ice-pans
and the sodium-lit boulevards
of Upper Ettingshall.

Maybe his thoughts
were the shadows no one sees
thrown up and down
beyond the whirligigs:
the black ache of boyhood Llanelli,
the shortest stint ever seen off
down Blaenhirwaun Big Vein,
heatless lodgings a smut's flight
from Dudley Castle,
learning to collar and funnel the volts,
Montevideo, Gib, being sunk twice
in the Indian Ocean.
A marriage slowly edging off
to join my sister,
dead at three days old.

Or perhaps he warmed himself
with one of his bits of everlasting song—
took himself South Of The Border
as hooded crows gave him welcome
on the Wolverhampton Road…
pictured himself unfurling
a red sail out over the sea
as the last shift readied its agonies
before the lone partridge found that tree
and thought, oh, might as well.

Sunday Morning

I am watching
my father angle a cut-throat razor,
its rasp augmented in the silence
of this arctic room. He grasps
its ivory handle, snow drifts
ploughed from tight drawn skin,
white foam sloughed into an enamel mug.
The blade clattered clean.

      Outside a robin brights
      the grey metal day,
      demented wind chimes
      jangle broken counterpoints.

This is our time, just us,
for once a truce declared downstairs,
we are allies with no words,
I watch him lather a white beard
before the mirror whose silver
is slipping away. Reflected side by side,
my owl-eyed gaze, his pigeon blink.

      He wipes blood berries
      from his throat,
      crimson wounds blooming
      in the enamel sink.

These I have Loved

Foundries spitting soot / chained ponies on nettled wasteland / Midland Red 272 / upturned boat bridges over the rainbowed canal / bag of chips 6d / markets illuminated by paraffin / bargains second hand & salvage / kids with hands and hair unschooled / the wisdom of shallow pockets /

Foundry workers in donkey jackets rank with swarf / Black NHS glasses thick lensed to ensure what was seen was certain / gloved hands twisted by arthritic pain / the knots and gnarls of working days / ancestral grains / ghosts lodged in coal dust seams /

Housewives in cotton paisley aprons / frilly straps / deep pockets for pegs & Opal Fruits / anonymous nylon housecoats / woollen headscarves / concertina rain bonnets / string bag at the grocers / Brook Bond Orange Label by the quarter pound / *do not ask for credit* /

Coneygree Foundry Christmas party / ice-cream & Bugs Bunny / dresses of cherry blossom tulle / gingham / polka dots / bow at the back / brown Start-rite sandals for school days at Tipton Green / mute estates with sinister garden gnomes / tiny triumphs in the Express and Star /

Old hats in oval boxes like candy striped cheeses / navy school skirt rolled up three times / grey gaberdine raincoat two sizes too big / initialled handkerchiefs / knee-length red boots / matching beret / headmistress freaking out / the surprise of suspender belts gangly as newborn lambs /

Dudley Castle / Dudley Zoo / a grandmother who knitted without a pattern / school jumpers / gloves / socks for walks on Sedgley Beacon / yellow & orange leaves like dots freed from a Seurat / a Fair Isle scarf waving its own goodbyes /

Pit Fodder

Arise drowsy sleeper to the grey-eyed
dawn   hobnails sparking on worn cobbles
the landscape laundered black.
    Trapped in the rib-caged wheel you descend
its umbilical reel   men hacking anthracite
lungs   men of grit and stone and steel
with picks to seek the Staffordshire Thick
feed furnace mouths   fill the pockets of *'better men'*.
    Workhouse boys then unwillingly thrust
into the dangers of pillar and stall   to endless dark
dreaming of girls   green fields once seen
pit fodder for one generation   trenches the next
mud crawlers   *ancient hags doubled*
no gas masks here   but the fear of death
lives measured in bags of coal
souls lost to that poisonous breath
Gas boys   Gas.

Ivyhouse Junction

Napton Pride
nods to Flower of Glasnevin

paint-embroidered cans hang portside
awaiting Victorian rain

buffer tyres ride the basin water
undulations in a toy Loch Ness

The Light of Jackfield hasn't been tended
lows like a cow full of ironbound milk

masts tilt and parry mid-basin
each with the direst journey to tell

a single swan
the sun's approbation prinking its neck

sails into the midst of it all
arresting the braggart clack of the masts
stilling The Light of Jackfield
going wide about for the Tyrley steps

a bike-boy on the marina
watches as it fashions its wake
of gusted leaves and coots and water-boatmen

as a child might stand
moon-eyed
quiver-mouthed
while eternity
with patient smile
explains itself

Many Mansions

the shepherdess
on the mantel
looks up to heaven

thinks about
the promise of a house
its many mansions

wonders if
there's a mansion for her
at least a room

once her soul
sheds her brass body
with a quicksilver tear

and if in fact
she will like sitting
fingers threaded

in boxy air
imagining others
pent adjacently

decorously walled
folded on themselves
stainless vesture

given that the life
for which she was made
was all about hills

bushes black with rain
sopping tresses
ewes pinned in thorn

and sky
lots of sky
and never a room

save the farmer's
of an evening
ale and repletion

candle-fire
miles away
over bony grass

from where she dealt
with blood
with real lambs dying

Intoxication

      It's all in the way you look at things
or so they say. I remember them being purchased
in a junk shop just behind The Miners Arms.
My hand went out instinctively to three silver
bottle tags, fingers tracing the engraving, *whisky,
gin, vermouth,* how they glinted in the forty-watt
light amongst tarnished soup tureens and discarded
cutlery, but oh, that word   vermouth!

      It was evenings in cerise silk pyjamas,
something louche, bohemian, a life away from corseted
cares. Listening to Rachmaninov, nights at the Royal Opera
not the sixpenny stalls at the Sedgley Clifton. No, the life
I deserved sitting in a green Lloyd-loom chair, wafting
about a Hampstead flat thin and mysterious, smoking
something sweetly scented. I would have written
a clutch of acclaimed collections, beautiful poetry
not the usual tat that is continually rejected.

      It's all in the way you look at things,
in the way one's hand reaches out for beauty,
a rose, a baby's hand, a moment of success,
and that word vermouth   is still   intoxicating.

Earless

'Brumas' 1957 - 1963

From a swollen sky,
one cloud lowers
to watch what we're at:
a crater,
two hacked, sloppy feet each way,
as though the nettles
had hollowed a throat
for their bitter voices.

At its rim
an earless teddy bear,
our three faces upswung
like the full moons of a whole new planet,
stunned at having to share any space
with whatever its world might know
in the way of drizzle and heaven's smoke.

Earless was my illness's escort.
Chickenpox, the word, takes up the same room
as Pepsodent, which trilled itself out of the telly
all the week my body burned
till I was handed back my peaceable skin.
(So did the name of Yuri Gagarin,
the only foreign words my parents spoke.)

Altar-server cousin pronounces:
now the plague is burrowing into my history,
the bear should show it the way.
His words, a furl of incense,
do not surprise me,
unlike his sister's non-congregant *Yeah!*

Here we are, then,
losing my lumped-over sidekick to Australia.
That snooping cloud lifts away at cousin's tone,
his Latin like the blague of a Hippodrome wizard.
I honestly expect a flash, Earless no more,
soil and nettles in place
like boot and spade never abused them.

But no: cousin raises Earless by the neck,
lies him belly down. We all shovel.
To start, the dirt is light rain on mahogany fur,
then roams into rashes.
And so he vanishes, the keeper of my greenest years,
along with my week of monstrous hurt—
like an errand-boy sent packing from a doorstep,
roped in sausages of manky grey.

Heirloom

Teddy, a Chad Valley original in toffee mohair,
fully jointed with pad paws and bought on tick,
two and six a week. Mum saved the bus fare,
walked the three miles home.

No picnics for him, never went down to the woods
but round and round the garden in the second-hand
Silver Cross pram with Netta the orange plastic doll,
her cracked skull Elastoplast repaired.

A trophy to successful motherhood after years
of empty arms, too precious for a *waspish wench*
who never quite matched the fantasy,
her stuffing too soon knocked out.

Teddy became a lasting heirloom, locked
in the oak closet, wrapped in his plastic
shroud, while I put away my accent,
caught the last bus home.

Unmapped

Here is a country road
blocked with rubble a few yards in
so it does not know
its journey any more
cannot call back sky and incident
from all the years

the buttoned feet
that tapped along it
Sundays in their close white chafe
petrol blush upon the leaves
when someone got out and got under
a Vespa lamp stinging the dusk

it cannot now look up
from its bends
at how tree-tops net the seasons
in stars of summer blood
and Christmas pearl

a bird sits on the rubble
looks inland
at the onwardness as was

the stroke on a map
each day more not there
sunk a touch deeper
through the tides of the earth

Baggeridge Wood

Gospel End Village, South Staffordshire

At the edge of the wood, I watch
as passing cars start to put on their lights.
Behind me, the fields of the closing year
sigh over and under. Bridleways
drift into each other, dogleg miles
for anyone who needs to walk unthinking.

A while back I was yards away
from a shaping flash—badger, fox,
or maybe a fairy-tale newly escaped
from some Christmas card still shining
in the moment between curtains drawn
and the first lamp of night—

yes, maybe a caroller
at the very back of an upholstered crowd
who sighed his last notes
all over the handsome snow
and left the wind to sing his silence.

Maybe a deer leaping higher than dreams
to land sure-footed among its own,
far from cuteness and rifle.
Or a special star making earthfall,
its message tattered in the mulch.

I listen. No sound from within the wood.
Still I stretch a hand. Even now
it might guide one more toneless murmur
of mothers mild and lowliness,
or speed a home-going flank,
or cup the downward fire
of one star less in all the everlasting.

Cats Fed

It's just something you do,
with all the litter training, the flea goo,
the last trip to the vets. You'd never think
of swapping notes that say *breath taken*
or *new thought dismissed.*

It seems so strange
to write it on that bit of desk calendar,
halved and torn off special
with its painting of the Rialto Bridge,
its motto about hope, small steps, sunrise.

I re-read the words as my hand's eyes
search my bag yet again
to check that all is as stuffed.
I've told the taxi to pick me up
two roads away—

don't want to give those other eyes—
in gate-posts, between curls of privet—
any cause for gossip. They'd get it wrong
and love it. Well, truth is such a let-down,
a cracker with only a loo-roll skin.

Outside I turn for a last look
at the house. For a moment
its windows burst into history—
birthdays, the heaping wakefulness
of Christmas, the sandcastle dreams—

then recover the face of mid-morning.
All at once I'm unfamilied. It's as if
the house is one I might have glanced at

on my way to someone's address
in a town I can hardly spell.

Somewhere in there they begin,
the little songs a house sings to itself
to ward off the fear that it's just
a geometer's whimsy. Pipes chuckle.
Clocks brew the top of the hour—

maybe too a stray catch of air
gets under that scrap of paper,
skews my final words on the life
I've locked—even bats them about
as cats might, full, frisky, uncaring.

Dog Collar

I buried the dog in its basket along with its bowl,
his tartan collar in my hands this morning
reminding me of the day when you said
I was too sentimental. We were sitting opposite
each other, riding the raft of our ring stained
table that even then was drifting towards

    another place. I buried thoughts of that bed bound
world, strip lit rooms highlighting the silver
in your hair, your voice swallowing itself, words
indigestible as hot bread. Afterwards, I never
gave your clothes away just let bin liners slump
like old drunks in the hall. Locked walking shoes

in a closet, unburied slews of paper, weak spined
love letters re-creased and folded without regret.
Let old words unknit themselves and drift aimless
into thin skies, the weight of them had lain too long
inside me. Now I am balloon light my face cerise blushed,
a small pomegranate with tempting pale pink flesh.

Jacqueline Burnett

Holy Trinity Roman Catholic School, Oxford Street, Bilston, 1958-1965

We were in the same class
at primary school. Shared
the same birthday. One year
were told to stand up
so the room could sing
and toast the nothing we'd done.

Slight, she was, freckled:
tawny keeps coming to mind.
Already bringing on a bit of a stoop
to oblige the future.

You'd glimpse her
slipping out to play,
edging the shadows
of the manager's son
and the town-clerk's daughter.

She answered each question perfectly
then retrieved her stillness,
putting the world away from her
till called upon again.

She rarely smiled,
perhaps never,
certainly not the day she and I
held an end apiece of coincidence,
like a pageant-flag
golden from a brush of sun
fluttered in a pocket of wind.

Sally Riordan

There was only the one world
and it was Sally Riordan's.
Fifty yards from her front door
to the school and each day
she made priceless work of it.
Hers was a nose for the good air high above,
a hand to summon in the shields and lions,
put a fan through its witching play.
She couldn't meet your gaze dead on—
her eyes would drift up to the blue lands
where Tony Curtis lived, where Diana Dors waited
to gift her a sample of Knight's Castile.
Royalty, Sally. Mum was the school's
chief cleaner, carpenter dad popped in to fettle
on his way to or from the big life.
To those of us who came out of the mists
a mile or more away, whose parents
worked on remote stars with vague orbits,
hers was a country of certain bounds
and charters. Once she turned up
in her slippers. When she realised,
she led our mirth, our handclaps to the brow,
let us into her Rubovia to play among its oaks.
You'd think that, for a few cloakroom minutes,
we'd tumbled a trunk of silks
in a place the colour of nothing.

(*A Rubovian Legend* was a children's television series which ran from the mid-50s to the early 60s, using marionettes for the characters.)

Mrs MacIntyre

The Bramford County Primary School   Coseley 1955 - 1975

More and more she thinks of her former calling.
Winters of grey sugar paper light   frozen milk
turn the handle duplicating   black stencils
greasy finger prints   worksheets placed cruciform
her head rushed with moment-to-moment busyness
how all that once defined her   creative lessons
magic sparking in bright eyed classrooms
nature tables   tadpoles   awe and wonder
look perfect snowflakes   hold out your hand
the staff room slew of books and half-eaten lunches
a pyramid of mugs in the filthy sink
sack race years   egg and spoon   nativity plays
giggling angels   goodbye summers
in her sleep breath rising to the rhythm
of tiny feet on the playground
in her hand another hand

in her hand another hand
tiny feet on the playground
in her sleep breath rising to the rhythm
of sack race years   egg and spoon   nativity plays
giggling angels   goodbye summers
pyramids of mugs in the filthy sink
the staffroom slew of books and half-eaten lunches.
Look perfect snowflakes   hold out your hand
nature tables   tadpoles   awe and wonder
magic sparking in bright eyed classrooms
how all that once defined her   creative lessons
a head rushed with moment-to-moment busyness
turn the handle duplicating   black stencils
greasy finger prints   worksheets placed cruciform
winters of grey sugar paper light   frozen milk.
More and more she thinks of her former calling.

Piano Teacher

You were a willow, sprouted from eau-de-nil paint,
your hands arching and lithe,
rain cold fingers tinkering a crazy ragtime.

You were Tuesdays always ready with a joke,
a quiet man pointing out the score,
every great beauty deserves flowers.

You were podgy as a new baked cottage loaf
granary hot, sometimes the pale ochre dough
stuck in the throat, the willow baton within reach.

You were the painted face of a grandfather clock,
your tinny chimes chuckling the hours, that great
pendulum with its deep-throated tocking.

You were Old Spice moments scored in the memory
when afternoon hours abandoned their stations,
sunlight chasing shadows across the lawn.

Diana Ingall

Diana Ingall was love and sweat.
Her hand-me-downs
kept warm the strain of generations,
including older sisters
who didn't properly exist
till *ample* and *pendulous* were coined.

She would expand with the school day
into the spaces left behind
by new tee-bar shoes and worked hems,
stare like the lady in the moated grange
at the flecks and cuts
of her far side of the table.

She lived by The Blue Boar
at the end of a broke-back row
and her brother would haunt the pub yard of a dusk
with his bits and bobs of America—
deck shoes, ebony quiff,
windcheater bunched
for the full thumb-and-beltloop thing.
So how's tricks? said the winks he'd scatter
at the landlord's bike, punished toilets,
nettles erasing a corner wall

till Diana arrived with the jug,
which he'd take in
and pass to her to hold steady
as they walked together home,
hoping that, for a spell of the night,
the beer would get dad out of Burma.

Nothing answered the brother's winks.
No one closed on Diana in kiss-chase.
Still he warmed the pub's gatepost,
still she never didn't smile
never didn't move like a mother
waiting only for the years and some bloke
and a niece's outgrown, wonky-spoked pram
to rise up, meet all the promises
of her endless heart.

What Granny Hayden had to Say

never step on the cracks my wench
live in fear of solitary magpies
avoid flash men with pumpkin smiles
miskin reared cocks always crow the loudest

a stitch in time saves nine
a fool and his money are soon parted
worry kills osses
just stop yer werriting

red headed women can't be trusted
birds of a feather flock together
like them at the back of Rackhams
a whistling woman and a crowing hen are neither good for God nor men

don't open your umbrella indoors   never walk under a ladder
money talks but it never speaks to us
when there's a new moon turn your money over
it' ll never appen   never in the rain of pigs puddin

go for cheap cuts   liver and kidneys brains and brawn
gut rabbits   pick out winkles   scrape the hairs off pigs' trotters
none of your fancy mouthing here
a blind mon on a galloping oss would be glad to see it   so should yow

Somersault

Batmans Hill Estate, Coseley, 1957-1972

Slowly I somersault through autumn.
The air is close but soft,
like the pillow you say goodbye to
at the nuzzle of sleep.
Now and then I reach a hand sideways,
catch hold again of times
no longer plunging about me…
moments, even. Here, now,
my fingers find the letterbox
of the family home.
Like a diver in a wreck,
I scull round the front door
to find Mum and Dad
argufying about which county
some crusted monument rears up in,
or who was on the phone just a minute ago
when it was live but silent.
Here's our Persian, alien butterball,
hauling its dust-whisk tail
round one of the downstairs gaps
that always seemed to be closing.
And there's Next Door of a sudden,
half in half out of the kitchen,
repeating she'll not stop,
pulling nightfall round her
like a revenant's cardie.

I tread space,
my hand now resting
on a slat of the Dutch airer,
breathe again the foundation smells
of tetchiness, uncorked Drambuie,

Sundays run to fat.
Then swing off,
back through the living-room's homage
to starburst fitments,
the wall-shelves interlocked
around souvenirs of cod-frolics
from places where they didn't talk like us—

till, rising past the windows
at all their archived pantomime,
I revolve at coping-height,
watch Him Across The Road
still tatting with the same car
he must have been born in.
Now my somersaults are slower yet,
revealing to my under-over eyes
the ancient grooves of municipal concrete
then the foundry-smoked crowns of trees—
and, just before I swing down again,
a glimpse of clouds
with muck-puddled bellies,
shepherding tails as thin
as a dopey apprentice
at the arse-kick start of the rest of his life,
forever dispatched for tools
that the fairies invented,
forever last to clock off,
turning his card round and round in the slot
till the doings takes pity and bites.

All the Light

At the rear of the nave
in a church down the way
from Coseley station,
a man holds fast
to all the light of the world.
He's not a praying man…
just took a fancy to light a candle
for all and several
on the way from work to train.
But the flame blew back,
billowing its grace around him
like a cloak from all the ages
succouring winter bones…
full of each sun that ever rose
on a tattered army, that ever set
on a gatepost mother
whose daughter kept on
not coming home.

What to do? If he moves a hand
it will mean dark snugging fast
to the limbs of Acapulco,
crofters falling sightless on the rocks
of Eigg, Lichfield with never a spire
to winnow the sky.
If he takes just one step
all the dawns to come
will simply fold in on themselves,
become a single star
ebbing through the Somerset levels,
melting down the barricadoes of Fez.

Someone must come, surely:
the vicar, set to lock emptiness
up with itself. A thief with
a niche taste in hassocks. Or perhaps
a saint, tired of the giddying beyond,
who will broach his ineffable radiance,
gather him away, reclothe him in
his homespuns…release him
hotfoot for the downline,
the change at Dudley Port,
the usual unremarked falter of day
over flats and ridge-runs,
the first of the streetlamps' coy fire.

Swimming Lesson Coseley Baths 1961

Once a week our class went swimming in that vast
bath of clear water without current or energy
of its own. We carried in rolled-up towels
and bales of cold air inside our hoods.

I liked to lose myself in the muffled depths
of the pool, below me restless light playing
on the bottom, forming and reforming
but never resolving. Fuzzy sounds echoing

off walls with blurred edginess. Our teacher's
barked commands almost silenced. Afterwards
in the changing rooms yelping classmates
and older women talking to no one in particular

about bodies reflected in steamy mirrors,
complaining about husbands, family, their many
small tragedies. Looking back perhaps the water
was not so clear but the trick was to keep swimming.

The Art of Knitting

My grandmother is wise, she can size
me up without a pattern, everything she knits
fits me to a T, pink cardigan, school jumper,
black mittens. Whole decades pass, she never
drops a stitch, as I grow and slip the matryoshka
shells, wool balls roll with the years. I am
spellbound by her fast ticking needles.
Knitting kept her old heart warm,
wrapped in rabbit wool she knew the art
of casting off the pull of memories.

knit one—purl one
knit two—purl two—cast on many more.

My grandmother knits bones into the best
of me, great cables rising up my chest,
safe sex advice knotted at the seams, focus
on reality not dreams, explains complex
Fair Isle design, fine two ply in ochre and green.
Do not wear red, do not go alone down twisted
paths that may never lead to home, some things
you cannot unpick, beware slick men with
a pumpkin grin, wear your cloak of homespun wool,
take care or your basket might never again be full.

knit one—carry one—turn
knit two—purl three—slip the last stitch over.

Local Vagrant   Dudley   1960's

Billy was that rasp of breath and curdling cough,
       a shadow man who preferred the depth of wasteland
and generous spread of nettles to dark hollowed doorways.

       You might find him along the canal with knitted shoulders,
heart and soul at their edge beside damp fires
       that neither lit nor warmed weighted days.

I wondered if he envied old oaks deep rooted
       in ferrous soil, wren and robin gone to their nests,
the lithe movements of willows?

Market days he begged near the War Memorial
       a bone bag man in a jacket that once fitted
a bigger self, yet something in him lead-potent

       like an unexploded mine. *Spare some change, mister.*
A man stepping the ledge of what is now and what
       was then, old news stories tight wrapped next to his skin.

Pity Phones

M. J. Thomas, SRN, Staffordshire and Dudley Health Offices, 1957-1974

District-nurse mother
so of course we had a phone.
Every third week she was on
emergency call.
Aged seven,
only just past the fancy
that whoever phoned us
must actually live
in the drawer of the phone-stand,
I found a new drama confecting itself:
pity in its hundred voices
halloo-ing my mother
down all the borough's threads.
I christened each
as it bodied out to me
from the one-sided talk:
Bad Fall, Pan Scald,
Playground Swing Chaos,
Head in Municipal Fence.

Till one night I heard her say
spina bifida, then *hmm, hmm, hmm*
like her voice
was coming gingerly downstairs—
and somehow knew without knowing
that here was a pity
done up proper and compact,
far above ragged-arse accidents
and the wee folk
who did but didn't live
in the country
beneath the phone.

Canal Bridge 236—Betsy's Tale

Night times she used to bring them here,
to the damp underside of upturned boat bridges
lit like a burlesque show. Wide mouth gaping men
echoing their little deaths into a hollow world
of fur coats and fish net tights. For years she spat barbs
kept throwing herself back into the same dark waters,
another scaly skin shrugged on, shrugged off.
She wanted the whole gamut of beauty, so kept
fishing, reeled in anything life had to offer.
236 was her childhood favourite where kind trolls
waited to grant wishes. Beside it, the corner shop
owned by *that foreign woman*, exotic smells
and bright blue pictures of the faraway she called home.
Fifty years later rotten planks are replaced by new.
A steel moon is netted in naked trees. Metallic light
on the canal still flickering that same hook
of promise.

Wyndham the Fuse: it Sure is

I still have his *Electrical Yearbook, 1966*.
Unfussy as the Book of Common Prayer,
calmly emphatic on insulation properties,
polyphase AC induction motors,
how to web and nurse domestic light.

Its cover is as green as Coseley Baths'
deep end. At the back, monochrome ads
for brushless alternators ('Quick response!'),
Potter's wirework, clip-on volt/ammeters—
all forever at fading-point, as though another book,

another year, needs to commandeer
their prudence. *Dad's,* I inscribed
at some point on the edge of its pages,
worried that some fine dawn
might find him stumped as to his trade.

One Thursday evening in the summer of the book,
he announced a shed clear-out. My mother
couldn't credit his sudden good sense:
'Tomorrow?' she asked, but he was out back already,
doing his shaman's jiggle with the lock.

Three journeys in his van to the plain of a tip
beyond Darlaston, and him with a joke
for every bend of the way. Each hummed
through his Glamorgan tenor
like the magic he worked with,

cowing it, making and breaking its flight—
as God might, I supposed, enthralled
by something He'd created while looking
the other way. *Casey said. This was too much
for the parrot. Then the Scotsman tries. Call me a cab.*

And his beloved: *Ahperader—Laws Angeles,
long distance. Yessir, it sure is.*
He repeated that one twice, three times,
then the reply, then just *it sure is*, as he steadied us
between the tip track's potholes and a sky

as deathly as a judge, rooftops
and chimney-necks crowding its robes
like poor-law cases. And again, *it sure is—*
calling back a different improbable magic,
Wembley's, England's:

*And the crowd are going wild! They think
it's all over!* Again the net wildly billowed.
It is now! ('Good show,' I remember him
muttering, obliged to support, as a mother might,
watching a neighbour's child on the swings.)

The shed never re-filled.
At the next World Cup, half-decimal,
half-deadweight coppers, Wales bumbled
and lost her voice again. Soon enough after,
he lost his.

Last time I went to Bushbury Crem,
I scouted for an hour in mortifying rain,
thought I had the place as clear
as a porch-and-kitchen circuit.
But he'd slipped through my assumption,

revealing its wires fatally unsheathed. I left the flowers
for an Amy Dabney, spinster, back by the gate.

It's all over. It is now. It sure is.

Authors

Michael W. Thomas has published ten collections of poetry, three novels and two collections of short fiction. His most recent poetry collection, prior to this, is *A Time For Such A Word* (Black Pear Press); his most recent short fiction collection is *Sing Ho! Stout Cortez: Novellas and Stories* (Black Pear Press); his most recent novel is *The Erkeley Shadows* (KDP / Swan Village Reporter). With Simon Fletcher, he edited *The Poetry of Worcestershire* (Offa's Press). His work has appeared in *Acumen, The Antigonish Review* (Canada), *The Antioch Review* (US), *The Cannon's Mouth, Critical Survey, Crossroads* (Poland), *Dream Catcher, Etchings* (Australia), *Irish Studies Review, Irish University Review, Magazine Six* (US), *Pennine Platform, Poetry Salzburg Review, The Times Literary Supplement* and *Under the Radar,* among others. He has reviewed for *The London Magazine, Other Poetry* and *The Times Literary Supplement*, and is on the editorial board of *Crossroads: A Journal of English Studies* (University of Bialystok, Poland). He was long-listed for the National Poetry Competition, 2020 and 2022, and long-listed and short-listed for the Indigo Dreams Spring Poetry Prize, 2023. For more information, please visit: www.michaelwthomas.co.uk
Blog, *The Swan Village Reporter*: http://swansreport.blogspot.com/

Poems by Michael W. Thomas
Dad in a Morning—December 1962
Ivyhouse Junction
Many Mansions
Earless
Unmapped
Baggeridge Wood
Cats Fed
Jacqueline Burnett
Sally Riordan
Diana Ingall
Somersault
All the Light

Pity Phones
Wyndham the Fuse: it Sure is

Tina Cole was born in the Black Country and now lives in rural Herefordshire near Ludlow. She has three published pamphlets, *I Almost Knew You*, (2018), *Forged* Yaffle Press, (2021) and *What it Was* Mark Time Books (2023).

As a poet and reviewer, she has led workshops with both adults and children and judged a number of U.K. and international competitions. Her published poems have appeared in many U.K. magazines and collections and one in The Guardian newspaper.

She is a past winner of a number of national poetry competitions 2010 – 2023 and completed an M.A. in creative writing/ poetry at Manchester Metropolitan University in 2023.

Poems by Tina Cole
Open the Box
Sunday Morning
These I have Loved
Pit Fodder
Intoxication
Heirloom
Dog Collar
Mrs MacIntyre
Piano Teacher
What Granny Hayden had to say
Swimming Lesson Coseley Baths 1961
The Art of Knitting
Local Vagrant   Dudley   1960's
Canal Bridge 236—Betsy's Tale

Acknowledgements

Tina Cole
Box 'Orbis' 207 (2024)
Knitting was highly commended in the Lord Whisky Poetry Competition (2023)
Music Teacher was highly commended in Phare/ Write Words Competition (2023)
Swimming 'Dreich' Magazine (2024)
These I have Loved was shortlisted in the Ver Poets Competition (2023)
Intoxication was long listed for the WOLF poetry Competition (2023)

Pit Fodder references *Dulce et Decorum Est* (Wilfred Owen, 1921)

Michael W. Thomas
Cats fed 'The Cannon's Mouth', Issue 91 (March 2024)
Jacqueline Burnett (as *Jacqueline Burdett*) 'Atrium Poetry' (May 2017)
Earlier versions of *Sally Riordan* and *Diana Ingall* 'The Poetry of the Black Country' (Offa's Press, 2017)
All the light was Commended in The Enfield Poetry Competition (2023)
Pity phones 'Coachlines' (2024)
Wyndham the Fuse: it Sure is 'God's Machynlleth and Other Poems' Flarestack (1996)

Reviews

Reviews of Michael W. Thomas's poetry:
'Finely crafted, thought-provoking poems, often reflective, sometimes humorous, but always arresting and original. Highly recommended.'
Neil Leadbeater 'Quill and Parchment' and 'Littoral Magazine'

'Michael W. Thomas's poems are rich with the details of past and present lives. They explore the widest—and wildest—possibilities of those lives with passion and humour.'
Alison Brackenbury

'The characters and landscape are brought to life in a series of finely crafted and thought-provoking poems, in which memories and insight fuse with curiosity and fascination for the world and its inhabitants.'
Alison Chisholm, Poetry Columnist, 'Writing Magazine'

Reviews of Tina Cole's poetry:
'Tina Cole invokes the landscape of her childhood in poems seething with rich imagery and forceful language.'
Helen Ivory

'These poems sing of the literal fabric of lives. I love the detail, texture and colour.'
Deborah Alma

'This attention to detail that's both familiar and sometimes unsettling, jolts us into a recognition of the secrets and subterfuges that shape lives...'
Deborah Harvey